the bath
gourmet

the bath
gourmet

by Rhonda Van

RUNNING PRESS
PHILADELPHIA · LONDON

9   8   7   6   5   4   3   2   1
Digit on the right indicates the number of this printing

Library of Congress Control Number: 2004090111

ISBN 0-7624-1827-3

Interior illustrations by Kelli Everett
Cover and interior design by Alicia Freile
Edited by Elizabeth Encarnacion
Typography: Ruzicka and Sassoon Sans

This book may be ordered by mail from the publisher.
Please include $2.50 for postage and handling.
But try your bookstore first!

Running Press Book Publishers
125 South Twenty-second Street
Philadelphia, Pennsylvania 19103-4399

Visit us on the web!
www.runningpress.com

For Tony

Who did not complain about beer in my hair, egg on the floor, chocolate powder in the towels, or the time I let the seaweed pot boil over and got seaweed all over the kitchen.

Contents

Introduction

Bathing is a ritual. First you run the water, at precisely the temperature that you, after a lifetime of experimentation, have deemed superior. Next, you may add some favorite ingredients, usually no more than a squirt of oil or bubble bath . . . though this book will help you with that part. Then, as the tub fills, you gather your supplies. These can range from the everyday to the outlandish—you may bring a notebook, a magazine, a candy bar, a cordless phone, even a pair of hand weights or a karaoke machine. The point is, it's a ritual for one, something tailored to exactly what you need to relax and steal some time for you alone.

So why aren't we taking more baths?

The ritual of bathing is thousands of years old. Civilizations around the world have used baths as part of their social life, religion, celebrations, and funerals. The Roman baths are the most famous, with their elaborate bathing houses that could accommodate thousands at once, as well as Warrior baths, frigidariums (check out the Polar Bear recipe if those intrigue you) and even baths with built-in libraries. Baths were also tremendously popular, both as recreation and ritual, to the Greeks, the Indians, the Turks, the Egyptians, and the Japanese. (Bathing went through a dark age of unpopularity later in history, when many doctors believed that baths caused consumption and nervous collapse, but fortunately those times are behind us.)

So, what happened? Today, despite our abundant bathtubs and available products (Icelandic Seaweed Mango—Enriched Bath Fizz!! Special Price This Week Only!!) most of us seem to be ignoring our tubs and jumping in and out of showers instead. We soap our bodies, scrub our hair, leap out of the shower and get on the run in four minutes flat. A bath, particularly a really fun or indulgent bath, is something we only think about taking on vacation . . . if even then.

Baths are worth the extra sixteen minutes. You can have that vacation experience every day, if you want. You don't need to send away for that Icelandic Seaweed Mango-Enriched Bath Fizz, either—this book will show that many of the most luxurious, spa-like baths are easily recreated at home, with ingredients you probably already have in your kitchen.

Try the ritual. It doesn't have to be all serious and flowery. You don't need aromatherapy and harp music to make a bath worthwhile. This book is for the rest of us, the people who prefer cookies to parsley rolls, hot chocolate to lychee tea. A bath is simply a slice of time custom-tailored just for you, with precisely what you need to relax and take that mini-vacation from regular life. I'll teach you the recipes that worked for me. Try them as they are, or use them as starting points for your own bath creations.

Enjoy.

To Calm Your Fears

(OR, BUT WON'T I GET STICKY, SMELLY, OR A HEADACHE TRYING TO CLEAN THE TUB AFTERWARD?)

The answer is no. But don't feel bad for asking—that's what everyone wants to know, and who can blame them? There's nothing luxurious about scrubbing out a tub full of gunk, accidentally dying your skin purple, or sitting around half the day waiting for a plumber.

Don't worry.

The secret to a disaster-proof bath recipe is to manage the proportions of your ingredients. For example, if you go wild and dump forty-nine boxes of gelatin powder into the bathtub trying to make a literal tub 'o Jello, then yes, you're going to have a mess to deal with afterward. However, if you add just enough powder to get the sensation without the solidity, you can enjoy the bath and the tub will drain with no trouble. Similarly, you would not be pleased with the results if you dumped a gallon of blue food coloring into your tub, but a few drops can give you the same tropical-blue bath experience (especially if you add some salt and plastic fish) without the drawbacks.

If you want to try a "starter" bath, look at the Cleopatra's Milk & Honey, Act Your Shoe Size, or Outdoor Bath recipes. If you prefer another recipe but are still nervous, try halving the ingredients the first time, or making your own version using the Bath à la Carte guidelines.

A few things to remember before you start:

ALLERGIES

Basic Rule: If you know it is unsafe to put something in your mouth, it is also unsafe to put it in your bath. If, for example, you are allergic to almonds, do not bathe in almond oil. Information about ingredient substitutions can be found in the appendices.

SKIN SENSITIVITY

Sometimes your skin will be sensitive to something that you're not allergic to when eaten. These recipes use mild ingredients to which few people have reactions. However, if you ever feel itchy or uncomfortable, get out of the tub immediately, rinse with fresh water, and don't use that ingredient again.

A special note regarding salt: a few unlucky people develop hives when exposed to water with very high salinity. The quantities of salt in these recipes are therefore kept low; if you're confident that your skin is not irritated by salt, go ahead and increase the quantities.

WOMEN

Any ladies with current gynecological concerns should always check with their doctors before adding anything to their bath water. (If all else fails, you can suggest an all-purpose soothing bath with a few tablespoons of baking soda, some candles around the tub, and someone to massage your aching shoulders.)

HAIR COLOR

Any coloring agent can be absorbed by hair, particularly color-processed hair. I recommend keeping your hair out of any color-tinted water.

PLUMBING

The ingredients in these recipes are not of the type or quantity that would be likely to cause clogs or other plumbing issues. However, since no one but you knows the quality of your pipes, it pays to proceed with caution.

OBLIGATORY DISCLAIMER

I'd be astounded if these recipes led to any bad experiences, but of course use your own best judgment in all cases.

Good-for-You Baths

(AS IN: BATHS THAT WILL DETOXIFY YOU,
EASE A SUNBURN, MAKE YOU SLEEPY,
WAKE YOU UP, MOISTURIZE YOU,
SMOOTH YOUR SCALY BOD, AND MORE!)

Fancy Herb Bath

— RENEW YOURSELF —

Sometimes we need to feel pampered for a while, just to balance out the grosser things in life. Promise yourself that for every yucky thing you have to deal with, you'll treat yourself to something good. Had to clean up after the neighbor's dog? You deserve a brownie. Parked under a pigeon nest? Ask someone for a foot massage. Something gray and slippery growing in the fridge? You need this bath.

The magnesium in the Epsom salt eases your muscles and helps scour anything nasty from your skin, while the rosemary and mint leave you feeling refreshed. If you have any other favorite herbs, you can throw them in as well. But the best thing about this bath is how simple it is; after the day you've had, simple is exactly what you need.

1 handful fresh rosemary   Other favorite herbs, if desired
1 handful fresh mint   ¼ cup Epsom salt

For steeping method: For boiling method:
A cheesecloth bag and string,   Medium-sized pot
   or a pair of clean nylons   Strainer

Bath mask

There are two ways to create this bath: boiling or steeping. Both are effective, so use whichever you prefer.

Steeping Method (easier): Open the cheesecloth bag or cut the foot off a pair of clean nylons, leaving enough extra material to knot the opening shut. Put the herbs into the bag, knot tightly if you're using a nylon or tie if the cheesecloth, and drop the bundle in a hot bath. This herb bag works like a teabag, so the water should be very warm. Add the salt to the water and stir. Without removing the herb bag, climb in the tub. The herbs release more fragrance the longer you soak.

Boiling Method (fancier): Add all the herbs to a medium-sized pot of water and cover. Bring to a low boil and simmer for about ten minutes. Cool the mixture, then strain, retaining the water. Pour the herbed-scented water into a warm tub, add the salt, and climb in.

Soak. Breathe. Tug on a bath mask and try to clear your mind. Continue soaking. Repeat as needed.

Cleopatra's Milk & Honey Bath

— SMOOTH AND SOFTEN SKIN —

The Queen of the Nile. Powerful. Gorgeous. She ruled a nation at a time when most women were lucky to be allowed out of the house. In her spare time, she confounded the Roman Empire and made lapdogs of its highest officers. Okay, maybe it wasn't her famous milk and honey baths that made it all possible, but then again, maybe it was.

Cleo wasn't alone in her love of bathing. Even everyday Egyptians bathed often, using oil to soothe away the ravages of the desert sun. They got the idea from the Greek philosophers, who promoted regular bathing in asses' milk for general health . . . though few people other than the queen could afford such luxuries.

Your own version of the bath will use cows' milk, but it's just as good for soothing and softening your skin. The honey and cornstarch are also great softening ingredients, so the combination of the three is the perfect thing if you're getting ready to seduce a Roman General.

INGREDIENTS:

⅓ cup cornstarch

4 cups whole milk or 1⅓ cups powdered milk

2 tablespoons honey

POWDERED MILK

If you want to use powdered instead of liquid milk in a recipe, use ⅓ cup of powdered for each full liquid cup the recipe calls for. For example, this recipe uses four cups of milk, so you'll need 1⅓ cups of powdered if you decide to substitute. **Note:** whatever you do, make sure the powder is fresh! If it is discolored or smells funny, throw it away.

GARNISHES:

Tray of olives

Natural sea sponge

Rose petals

Bare-chested bath attendant
(to sponge your toes while you
nibble olives, Cleopatra-style)

This bath is best enjoyed warm, but not hot. Add cornstarch into the running water, reaching underwater to see if any lumps have formed at the bottom of the tub; if so, just rub them for a moment and they'll dissolve. Then add the milk, also under the faucet. Add the honey last; the easiest way to add honey is to squeeze it from the bottle into your fist, then squeeze your fist under the running faucet until the honey dissolves.

Climb in the tub and gloat. Twenty minutes is about all you need for the smoothest and softest skin ever—in the meantime, shout a few commands. Eat olives. Have your attendant sponge your toes and scatter some rose petals on the floor for you to tread on as you leave the tub; Cleopatra was also famous for her love of roses. This is how it feels to be a living goddess.

CLEOPATRA'S HONEY MASK

Mix a tablespoon of honey into a cup of plain yogurt. Slather onto your face, leave on for ten minutes while you bathe, then rinse. The yogurt/honey mixture will leave your skin soft and moisturized, and honey is a natural astringent and antiseptic as well.

Turbo Tub

Need to get moving? If you're having one of those mornings where you have twenty-three things on your To Do list, but feel too droopy and blah to even tug on your sweatpants, haul yourself over to the tub and let this quick bath help you get started in style. The baking soda will refresh you, and the honey and grapefruit both have stimulating effects. As a bonus, you can always count on the smell of the grapefruit to give you an extra push!

Get in, get out, and get everyone out of your way.

3 tablespoons honey
1 grapefruit
2 tablespoons baking soda

Knife

Cup of coffee

Start running the bath, no warmer than body temperature. Add the honey by squeezing it directly from the bottle into your fist, then squeezing your fist under the running faucet until the honey dissolves. Cut the grapefruit in half, pick out the seeds, and then squeeze the juice into the tub. Add the baking soda last. If you want an extra jolt, leave a cup of coffee on the side of the tub to sip while you bathe.

Enter and enjoy, but don't expect to stay in the tub long; the ingredients in this recipe have a sneaky energizing effect. This isn't a recipe to try when you only want to relax. Just enjoy the bath and be on your way—and try to remember to put on some clothing before you dash out and climb a mountain.

Big City Bath

It's time to detoxify. Most of us live day after day with dirty air, pesticide-laden food, and who-knows-what in our water. Smog. Smoke. Perfume in a cramped elevator. And even if you don't live in a city, you can't truly escape all the pollutants seeping into your skin every day—at least not if you rely on mere soap and water. Sometimes you need to detoxify your skin, get that funny gas station smell out of your hair and leave yourself squeaky clean and ready to face those city streets again.

The oranges, grapefruit, and lime in this recipe are all filled with skin-loving vitamin C, while the baking soda refreshes you and keeps the water from becoming too acidic. The real secret, though, is the unbeatable soothing and detoxifying powers of the mustard powder. Think of this bath as an application of a traditional mustard plaster . . . everywhere at once!

1 heaping tablespoon mustard
  powder
2 oranges
1 grapefruit

1 lime
4 tablespoons baking soda
Baby bath bubble solution, if desired

Knife

Bath scrubber or mitt

Add the mustard powder and baking soda to a running bath. Cut the oranges and grapefruit in half and squeeze the juice into the tub. Cut the lime into circular slices and float the slices in the water. Add a splash of bubble bath solution if you want an extra treat. Enter the tub and soak. Rub a lime slice anywhere your skin feels especially dry, flaky, or scaly, then scrub, scrub, scrub with the bath scrubber or mitt.

Soak for at least twenty minutes to get the full effect, finish with a final application of lime slices to problem areas, then rinse with plenty of fresh water. Bundle up in a big white towel and enjoy how unpolluted you have become.

MESS ALERT

Seeds in the drain are no fun. It's a good idea to pick out the orange and grapefruit seeds before squeezing them into the bath water.

Drowsy Bath

— EASE INSOMNIA —

Warm milk didn't work? Too keyed up to count sheep? If you can't sleep, there's nothing worse than just thrashing around in bed and staring at the clock all night. A lavender bath is an old-fashioned cure that just might do the trick; the scent of lavender is known to be soothing and to make people drowsy. Your great-grandma was probably given lavender baths as a child to help put her to sleep, or she might have had a bundle of lavender sewn into her pillow. (But think about it: a bath is much nicer than dried herbs crunching under your ear.) Besides, while you're waiting for the lavender to take effect, a bath is a glamorous way to fill those wee hours.

INGREDIENTS:

1 large handful lavender (fresh or dried)

2 cups milk or ⅔ cup powdered milk

UTENSILS:

For steeping method:
A cheesecloth bag and string, or a pair of clean nylons

For boiling method:
Medium-sized pot
Strainer

GARNISHES:

A book. (Think slow-paced and epic, not vampires or car chases.)

INSTRUCTIONS:

There are two ways to prepare the lavender. Both are effective, so take your pick.

Steeping Method: Find a cheesecloth bag or cut the foot off a pair of clean nylons, allowing room to knot the opening shut. Put the lavender in the bag, tie or knot it shut, and drop the bundle in a hot bath. Hot water (but not scalding) is important to bring out the lavender, similar to using a teabag. Add the milk and climb in. The lavender water gets stronger the longer you soak.

Boiling Method: Boil the lavender for five minutes in a medium-sized pot of water. Allow to cool, then strain, retaining the water. Pour the scented water into to a warm bath. Add the milk. Climb in.

Now, just breathe. Close your eyes and picture something relaxing. Imagine you are riding in the back of a car on a long highway, watching the power poles go past the window, one after another. Or imagine you're lying on the grass near a windmill, watching those big arms slowly spin around and around. Or just read a book until you start to feel groggy.

When you start to feel seriously sleepy, leave the bath and go back to bed. It's unsafe to sleep in the tub; you could slide down and inhale water, or hit your head on the side of the tub, or get chilled as the water cools off. You'll be better off, and warmer, back under the covers.

USEFUL TIP

Paperbacks are easier to manage in the tub than hardcovers, and cheaper to replace when you accidentally drop your book into the water. Your bookmark will also likely take a plunge into the tub sooner or later, so try substituting a strip of tinfoil to mark your place.

Bigfoot Bath

— TREAT YOUR FEET —

Want to do your feet a favor? Whether you've just finished a day of holiday shopping at the mall, a Saturday hike, or even a charity marathon, the result is usually the same: a pair of feet that are ready for some serious pampering. You need to soak them in something cheerful and soothing. Immediately.

The cool water in this foot soak decreases swelling and helps shrink blisters, while the baking soda gets rid of that scary foot smell. Best of all, with a little forethought you can do this soak just about anywhere, any time you need some instant foot relief.

INGREDIENTS:

1 heaping cup baking soda   Liquid soap
⅓ cup light oil

UTENSILS:

2 sturdy gallon-sized plastic bags or 2 buckets, if using recipe away
  from bathtub

INSTRUCTIONS:

There are two variations to this bath, one for soaking your feet in the bathtub and another to use when you're on the go, such as at a campsite or a park. The recipe works great either way.

With a tub: Run a bath of cool to tepid water. Add the baking soda, oil, and five or six good squirts of liquid soap under the faucet. Turn off the water when the tub is a quarter full, sit on the edge, and stir the bath with your feet.

Without a tub: Find a hose or a water faucet and half-fill 2 gallon-sized plastic bags or buckets, then split any of the ingredients you have available—baking soda alone will do in a pinch—between them. Hold the bags closed and shake to mix, then open partway and put one foot in each bag.

Soak your feet, but don't scrub. Swish your feet in the soapy water, enjoy the oil, and let the cool water prepare your feet for your next adventure.

Banana Bath

The jungle beckons. Just for a little while, let yourself forget your shopping list, your e-mail, your dentist appointment. How long has it been since you practiced your jungle yell? Your primitive self is waiting, and it probably has better skin than you do.

Bananas are great vitamin-filled moisturizers, though very difficult to add directly to bath water without making a mess. In this case, the peels are used to scent the water, putting you in a jungle mood while the bananas themselves are reserved for a banana facial. This is one of the more complicated recipes, but if you love bananas and your skin is howling for moisture, you'll be glad you tried it.

INGREDIENTS:

Peels from 2 or 3 bananas	Baby oil, if desired
2–3 capfuls banana extract	Heavy moisturizing lotion

Medium-sized pot
Strainer

Bring four cups of water to a boil in a medium-sized pot, then add the peels from two or three bananas. Cover. Boil for six minutes, then remove from heat and allow to cool. Discard the peels and strain if necessary.

Add the banana-scented water to a warm running bath, then pour two or three capfuls of banana extract under the tap. If you're a fan of baby oil, add a splash of that as well.

Climb in and practice your jungle yells. Put on your Easy Banana Facial. Slather heavy moisturizing lotion onto your hands, elbows, feet, and ankles, and prop them on the rims of the tub while you soak. If you want the banana scent to linger on your skin, skip the baby oil and don't rinse when you're finished bathing.

EASY BANANA FACIAL

Laugh lines? Frown lines? Stayed-Out-Much-Too-Late Lines? Whatever you call them, you have three choices. You can live with them, spend half your paycheck on lotions and injections, or try this easy facial. Take a banana and mash it with about two tablespoons of milk. Spread the mixture on your face, neck, and shoulders while you're in the bath (so drips won't matter) and rinse it off when you're finished bathing.

Oatmeal Bath

An itch can drive you crazy. Allergies. Mosquito bites. Dry skin. Poison Ivy. Big dogs that lick your arms all night, so you wake up caked with drool. Whatever it was that started your itching, an oatmeal bath is a great way to make it stop. Oatmeal is an ancient remedy that has, in modern times, gained medical respect for its miraculous ability to calm itchy skin. It also acts as a natural exfoliant, so while you are soaking you can also use it to scrub away some of the impurities that started the itching in the first place.

By the way: you don't have to wait until you itch to try this one. An oatmeal bath is also a good idea if your skin feels fine but you're feeling homesick for the oatmeal your grandma used to make you eat.

MAKE IT STRONGER

If you're **really** itchy (and have already consulted with your doctor about the reason) you can make this bath stronger by blending the oatmeal into a coarse powder before starting the bath. This takes just a second or two in a regular blender. You can also add a tablespoon of cornstarch to the mix, for extra soothing power.

1 cup uncooked oatmeal

Thin, knee-high nylon sock or clean pair of old nylon hose

Cinnamon-scented candle

Pour one cup of uncooked oatmeal into a knee-high nylon sock, or cut the foot off an old pair of nylons at knee height and pour the oatmeal in there. If you like, light a cinnamon-scented candle for that cinnamon-oatmeal smell. Hold the neck of the sock over the faucet and run a warm (not hot) bath, filtering the water through the oatmeal. When the bathtub is full, enter and soak. Make an oatmeal ball by tying a knot in the sock, then wring the excess fluid into the tub. Use the ball like a sponge, rubbing it over your arms and legs, under your chin, between your toes, anyplace that feels less than perfect. Rinse with cool water when you're finished.

MESS ALERT

Don't let go of the oatmeal bag while the water is running, and don't try tying or rubber-banding it to the faucet unless you're willing to clean up **a lot** of scattered oats when the bag does the inevitable and slips off the tap.

WHAT TO DO WITH A SOCK FULL OF OATMEAL

Since you already have wet oatmeal you might as well use it to do something good for your face. Cut the sock from the Oatmeal Bath recipe open and mix half the oats (about a half cup) with a half cup of plain yogurt. Spread the mixture on your face, read a magazine article or two, then wash away with cool water. (This also works if you just use one-half cup regular uncooked oatmeal—no sock required.)

Sunburn Soak

You fell asleep while lounging beside the pool. Or you forgot to bring your sunscreen to the beach. Or maybe it took a lot longer than you expected to get the barbecue going. Whatever happened, you spent too much time in the sun and you're suffering now. This recipe takes the edge off your sunburn pain and helps your skin start to recover.

Sunburned skin is inflamed skin, and few things help inflammation better than black or chamomile teabags; at the same time, cool (and also anti-inflammatory) cucumber slices will be soothing the worst of the burns.

SELF HYPNOSIS

The less often you have to take this bath, the better. Sunburns are very unhealthy. Too much unprotected sun exposure can lead to wrinkles, premature aging of your skin, and even skin cancer. Spend some of your time in this bath closing your eyes and practicing self-hypnosis, to help you remember not to end up in this sad situation again. Try reciting the following mantra:

Baking is for bread . . .
I am not bread.
Baking is for bread . . .
I am not bread.

INGREDIENTS:

1 cucumber
½ cup cornstarch

6–12 teabags for black tea
or chamomile tea

UTENSILS:

Knife

GARNISHES:

Ice cream
Grice

A hot bath would broil your sunburn right now, so fill the tub with tepid water. You can always add a jolt of warm water later if you start to get a chill. Cut the cucumber into slices and put them within arm's reach of the tub. Pour the cornstarch under the running tap, then reach underwater to rub away out any cornstarch bumps that may have formed at the bottom of the tub. Add the teabags next, then ease yourself into the bath, submerging as much of your aching body as possible. Layer the cucumber slices on anything burned that is still above water—the tops of your shoulders, your cheeks, your nose. Finally, place a cucumber slice on each eyelid and try to relax. You need at least twenty minutes for the anti-inflammatory effects of the teabags to work. In the meantime, enjoy some ice cream or grice and get yourself into a cooler mindset.

GRICE

Still feeling overheated? Remove a bunch of seedless grapes from the stem, rinse them, pat them dry, then put them in the freezer overnight. (Be sure to use seedless grapes—frozen grapes are tasty, but frozen seeds are not.) Once frozen, the grapes make great treats to carry around in your mouth on a hot day or when you're trying to get in a cooler mindset.

Broadway Bath

— HELP A COLD —

It's hard to see the bright side of having a cold, with sniffling, sneezing, sinus headaches, and all. The truth is that there is no cure for a cold, but at least you can help the symptoms: warm water soothes your achy body, and breathing steam breaks up the goop in your sinuses, especially when mixed with the tart smell of lemon. Lemon and honey are both time-honored cold soothers, so think of this bath as a full-body variation!

If you're very lucky, you'll take this bath on that certain morning, halfway through the cold, when the sore throat is suddenly gone and you're left with that husky, sexy, superstar voice that you secretly wish would last forever. It's the perfect time for singing in the bathtub, the best acoustical spot in the house. But don't worry if you're not so lucky—you can always skip the singing and cheer yourself up with some favorite Broadway soundtracks instead.

INGREDIENTS:

2 tablespoons honey   3 tablespoons baking soda
3 lemons

MESS ALERT

You don't want lemon seeds down the drain. It's easier to pick them out of the lemon halves **before** squeezing than it is to pick them out of bath water after.

The Bath Gourmet

Broadway music

Before running the bath, you need to breathe some steam. Close the bathroom door and run only the hot water for a few minutes, allowing it to drain. Once the mirror is fogged up, close the drain and start running a warm bath. Add the honey by squirting it into your fist and then holding your hand under the faucet while squeezing the honey until it dissolves. Add the baking soda next. Finally, cut the lemons in half and squeeze the juice under the running faucet. You can also float the squeezed lemon halves in the water, if desired. Don't worry about pulp—they float very neatly rind-side-down. Soak a washcloth and drape it over your face to really help reduce your symptoms. Now, if your throat isn't sore, you can enjoy that voice while it lasts. Sing! Play some music as accompaniment if you like, or invite someone in to be a backup singer. Try show tunes, movie tunes, or anything else that properly showcases that sexy, throaty, husky voice of yours.

UPSIDE-DOWN LARYNGITIS CURE

Heat up about two cups of water on the stove, squeeze in the juice from one lemon, and add a big squirt of honey. Now dangle upside down off the arm of the couch or the edge of the bed and drink. The extra effort of swallowing upside down will make the solution coat your throat much more thoroughly.

Seaweed?
Yes, Seaweed Bath

— ALL IN ONE: DETOXIFY, ENERGIZE, MOISTURIZE —

Who needs a seaweed bath? This is a bath for multi-taskers, especially multi-taskers with sore muscles and dry or irritated skin. If you're the kind of person who demands a single all-purpose hair product instead of five, who sorts the mail while talking on the phone, and who plans to be updating your appointment book while taking this bath, then this is the recipe for you.

Seaweed is a multi-tasker, just like you. First, it's loaded with minerals, which work to unkink your muscles, detoxify you, and exfoliate your skin.

Second, it's filled with natural oils to leave you soft and touchable. The extra minerals in the Epsom salt add punch to the first part, while the oil in the recipe boosts the moisturizing effect of the second.

Truthfully, this is not an attractive bath—but the benefits are worth it. Just put away your appointment book for a few minutes, bathe by candlelight, and pretend you are in an extremely expensive spa.

INGREDIENTS:

2 sheets dried seaweed

½ cup Epsom salt

1 tablespoon sesame oil

INGREDIENT NOTE

Ask for sheets of dried seaweed in the market. It is inexpensive, and there will probably be recipes on the wrapper to help you convert the leftover sheets into sushi or seaweed soup.

UTENSILS:

2 medium-sized pots

Strainer

GARNISHES:

Candles

Plastic fish

INSTRUCTIONS:

Fold two sheets of dried seaweed into quarters. Bring three cups of water to a slow boil, then add the seaweed. Reduce heat and simmer, uncovered, for six to seven minutes, then remove from the heat. This mixture will not look remotely appealing, but don't panic—you're not done yet.

The seaweed will have dissolved into a blackish-green mass. Strain the seaweed mixture into another container, retaining the liquid. It will take several minutes in the strainer to separate the water fully. Discard the strained seaweed mush and add the purple-tinted liquid to a bathtub filled with warm water. Add the salt and sesame oil.

For full detoxifying and moisture-building benefits, soak for at least twenty minutes. Spend the time gloating. Think of all those people who are, right this minute, paying hundreds of dollars to have themselves wrapped head-to-toe in seaweed. They are feeling slimy and a little embarrassed right now, while you are enjoying the privacy of your tub. Rinse with clean water when you're done, and enjoy.

SALT SCRUB

Still have old, dead skin that needs to be sloughed off? In a shallow bowl, mix equal parts salt and baby oil. Rub the mixture in circles on any particularly scaly parts, then rinse.

Turkish Bath (Hamam)

— ULTIMATE CLEANSING —

There's only one ultimate bath, and it's the Turkish version. Are you ready for the total spa experience? You don't need a plane ticket, just a little time.

For thousands of years, the Hamam has been an essential part of Turkish life; a place to socialize, to relax, and to celebrate everything from births to weddings. Turkish baths have been prescribed to cure headaches, earaches, arthritis, and even old age. Whether those work for you or not, one thing is certain: you'll never feel cleaner, or sleep better, than after enjoying a traditional Turkish bath.

A friend recently went to an authentic Hamam near Istanbul. Her description:

"You go in the bathhouse, and you feel like you've gone back in time. It's an old marble room, and it's incredibly humid. The walls are sweating. There are all these ferocious old women wearing nothing but giant black underwear, and they scrub you with soap and a piece of burlap. This is no gentle cleansing! In the middle of the room is a circular marble slab, and you lie there for a massage. It's more like being pummeled than gently kneaded."

INGREDIENTS:

1 bundle mint leaves
Mild liquid soap

Moisturizing lotion

UTENSILS:

Large bowl for pouring water (tas)
Large bath mitt, loofah, or
  bath scrubber (kese)

3 large towels (pestimal).
  Traditional pestimal are
  usually striped or checked.

GARNISHES:

Turkish apple tea (elma kayi)
  if you can find it, or other
  favorite tea
Fresh fruit

Bath attendant to do the massaging
(traditionally should be same-sex,
but any significant other will
work fine).

INSTRUCTIONS:

It starts with steam. Close the bathroom door, remove your clothes, and run the shower very hot (don't enter the shower) until your mirror is completely fogged with steam. Now run a hot—but not painfully hot—bath. Crush the mint leaves and drop them in the water, then soak for fifteen minutes. Relax and enjoy the mint smell while your pores open and your skin softens.

After fifteen minutes, you're ready to begin the process. Stand up in the tub, fill your bowl (tas) with cool water, and pour it over your head and body. Repeat twice. Sit on the edge of the tub and scrub like crazy with the mitt or loofah (kese), using soap. Scrub as hard as you can without causing pain. Scrub all over, except your face. Start with your heels and move up. This will take a while, but keep at it. Well-exfoliated skin really does feel like velvet once you're finished.

Wash your face and hair as you normally would, then fill your bowl with more cool water and start pouring again. Rinse everything thoroughly before stepping out of tub and wrapping yourself in your towels (pestimal). The traditional wrapping method is one towel on your head, turban-style, one around your shoulders, and one around your hips.

Rest, sipping your Turkish apple tea (elma kayi) or another tea, and snacking on fresh fruit. When you're ready to move on, the massage begins—rub moisturizer everywhere you scrubbed, kneading your muscles as you go. If you can recruit an attendant, ask for a firm, deep, all-over massage as the moisturizer is applied. Re-wrap yourself in the towels and have another cup of tea. You're finished, and as clean and smooth as you'll ever be without taking this bath all over again . . . or going to Turkey.

Recipe Title:

Purpose:

Description:

Ingredients:

Utensils:

Garnishes:

Instructions:

Recipe Title:

Purpose:

Description:

Ingredients:

Utensils:

Garnishes:

Instructions:

Recipe Title: _____

Purpose: _____

Description: _____

Ingredients: _____

_____

Utensils: _____

Garnishes: _____

Instructions: _____

_____

_____

_____

_____

Recipe Title: _____

Purpose: _____

Description: _____

Ingredients: _____

_____

Utensils: _____

Garnishes: _____

Instructions: _____

_____

_____

_____

_____

Fun Food Baths

(AS IN: BATHS TO TRY IF YOU LOVE
CHOCOLATE, MAPLE SYRUP, JELLO,
SPICES, NUTS, ETC.)

Make Me
Irresistible Baths

— THRILL SOMEONE —

Sometimes perfume just isn't enough. If you're looking to drive someone wild, the scents people respond to most are food. Vanilla. Maple syrup. Cinnamon. Root beer. Try marinating yourself in one of these food-scented tubs, and be ready to accept a lot of attention from your significant other. Or take one of these fragrant baths to remind you of one of your favorite treats from childhood. Either way, these simple soaks are sure to please!

Choose any of the bath flavors listed below. Add a few capfuls of unscented bubble bath to the mix to make the tub more attractive—especially if there will be witnesses—but remember that these baths are intended to smell better than they look!

Root Beer Delight

INGREDIENTS:

1 drop root beer concentrate   Unscented bubble bath, as desired

INSTRUCTIONS:

Be prepared—root beer concentrate is extremely concentrated. One drop is enough to scent your bath; much more than that will scent your entire neighborhood. Add the drop (or two, if you're daring) to a hot bath and soak. Dab a teeny-tiny bit of concentrate behind your ears before you get out.

Cinnamon Bun Soak

INGREDIENTS:

2–3 capfuls vanilla extract
4 cinnamon teabags (not for use if pregnant.)
Unscented bubble bath, as desired

INSTRUCTIONS:

Add two or three capfuls of vanilla extract under the tap of a hot running bath, get in, and float the cinnamon teabags around you as you soak. Be warned that cinnamon doesn't dissolve well, so you may have to splash a little cinnamon residue out of the tub after you drain the water.

Pancake Lover's Tub

1–2 capfuls imitation maple flavoring
Unscented bubble bath, as desired

Add one or two capfuls of imitation maple flavoring to a hot running bath. Maple flavoring can be found in the baking section of your grocery store, near the spices and food coloring. The maple flavoring will make the bath water look dirty, so use bubbles to hide the color. The maple-scented bath water is also great for dabbing behind your ears or as a final rinse for freshly-washed hair.

Sushi Bath

This is the bath to take if you are feeling unappreciated. Are other people failing to notice your charm, your brilliant wit, the five pounds you lost? Do you get the feeling that even if you gave them your time, your best efforts, your kidneys, they would never even say "thank you"? Just think—if you were a member of ancient Japanese royalty, they would have to bow to you. They would never dare give you as much as a nasty look. They would have to serve you tea and fluff your blankets. And they would have to draw you this bath.

1 cup uncooked white rice   2 teaspoons sesame oil

Seaweed soap
Pair of nylon hose, or a thin knee-high nylon sock

Floating candles   Relaxing music

This is an unconventional version of a conventional Japanese bath. Therefore, in keeping with tradition, don't even think about getting into this bath until you've scrubbed yourself thoroughly in the shower—it is barbaric to allow any soap suds into the bath water. Use seaweed soap; it will put you in the sushi mood, and it also is rumored to have miraculous fat-melting properties. No harm in trying it.

Pour one cup of uncooked white rice into the foot of an old, clean pair of nylons cut off at knee height, or a thin nylon sock. Run a very hot bath (but not scalding) as deep as your tub will allow, putting the opening of the sock over the faucet so the water runs through the rice as it fills the tub. Add two teaspoons of sesame oil to the water. The point of this bath is to melt away stress, so play relaxing music and add some floating candles if you think they'll help.

When the tub is full, remove the nylon sock from the faucet and tie a knot to securely close the rice bag. This homemade bag makes a gentle yet effective loofah, and smells so good you will be tempted to take a nibble, but don't. Rub the bag behind your ears instead, and maybe later someone will nibble on you instead.

MESS ALERT

Pouring rice into the foot of a nylon is a little trickier than it sounds. Don't do it on your partner's side of the bed.

Chocolate Mud Bath

— CALLING ALL CHOCOLATE LOVERS —

Pine trees rustling overhead. A wood-rimmed outdoor tub. Warm mud ooz-
ing between your toes and enveloping you all the way up to your earlobes.
A mud bath sounds like heaven, but the truth is, you don't want real mud
in your bathtub. It would make a mess and put horrible clogs in your drain.
Plus, it would probably stink up the bathroom. On the other hand, a chocolate bath gives you the look of a mud bath, the benefits of a milk bath, and
the smell of chocolate. One of my favorites.

INGREDIENTS:

3 cups milk

Chocolate powder or syrup
  for making chocolate milk

⅓ cup cornstarch

2 tablespoons vanilla,
  or 2 tablespoons rum

Pitcher or mixing bowl   Long-handled spoon

Ice cream sandwich

Pour the milk into a pitcher or mixing bowl and stir in enough chocolate syrup or powder to make very rich chocolate milk, following the package instructions. Don't be afraid to add a little extra chocolate; the milk should be a nice, dark color when you're finished.

Pour the mixture into a warm, running tub. Add the cornstarch. If you prefer a bath with more chocolate scent or a darker color, add another batch of chocolate milk. Two tablespoons of vanilla extract or rum will give the bath an extra kick. Slide in and inhale. Imagine yourself at an expensive spa, getting a full body mud treatment. Remember, the water is supposed to be brown—it's a mud bath. Actually, this is essentially a milk bath with a sense of humor, so eat your ice cream sandwich and laugh a little.

MESS ALERT

Never put chocolate powder directly into the bath water without stirring it into milk first, because it won't mix properly and will leave powder residue all over your tub. You also don't want to risk spilling the box of powder into your bath mat!

Cannibal Bath

— BASTE YOURSELF IN SPICES —

The idea behind a marinade is to soak something in a special spice solution to make it even more tender and delicious. If it works for lamb chops and prime rib, why shouldn't it work for you?

And, really, who doesn't want to be just a little bit more tender and delicious?

INGREDIENTS:

Fist-sized chunk of fresh ginger

2 fat pinches dried orange peel

1 cinnamon teabag (not if pregnant)

INGREDIENT NOTE

If you can't find dried orange peel in the store, you can substitute two fat pinches of grated fresh orange peel instead.

UTENSILS:

Blender

Old, clean pair of nylons, or thin knee-high nylon sock

GARNISHES:

Plate of ginger spice cookies or sugar cookies

CUKE HEAD

As long as you're marinating your body, you might as well do your head at the same time. To super-moisturize your hair and face, blend half a cucumber with one egg. Apply about a half of this mixture to your face. Use your finger to stir two capfuls of your favorite conditioner into the rest and work it through clean hair. Leave on throughout your bath, then rinse.

INSTRUCTIONS:

Drop the ginger into a blender and blend on the gentlest setting for a few seconds. Stir in the orange peels and put the mixture into the cut-off foot of an old, clean pair of nylons or a nylon sock. Hold the opening of the nylon packet over the faucet, so the water runs through the spices as you run a hot bath.

Climb in and marinate. Float a cinnamon teabag in the water. When the tub is full, tie a knot in the top of the sock and drop it in the water like a teabag. Ginger is stimulating, so you may end up deciding to pop out of the tub to go jogging within twenty minutes or so. In the meantime, it's time to choose: if the spicy bath brings out your spicy side, yell for some company and share a plate of ginger spice cookies. If you prefer more of a sugar-and-spice balance, eat the sugar cookies instead.

MESS ALERT

If you don't have fresh ginger, don't try to substitute the pink kind served alongside takeout sushi. Its smell is all wrong and it looks horrible if it gets loose in the water.

Nutty Bath

— GO NUTS —

Remember when you were a kid, and you and your best friend made up nonsensical games? Only the two of you truly understood all the crazy rules. Your favorite might have been something like the Game of Count Oog: you would run to the tree on the end of the yard, screaming "I am Count Oog Oog Oog!" then run and touch something orange, then sprint into the house and leap on the couch, screaming, "I am Count Oog Oog Oog!" "No, I am!" "No, I am!" "I am!" Then you would do it all over again. No one else in the world understood you, and that was part of the delicious fun of it, what made it so silly and wild and great.

This bath is like that. With hundreds of walnuts floating in the tub like tiny bath toys, you'll soon be inventing silly games to play with them, guaranteed. The walnut extract, almond oil, and vanilla will create a nutty aroma to complement the fun.

INGREDIENTS:

3–5 pounds unshelled walnuts

2 tablespoons almond oil

2 capfuls black walnut extract

2 capfuls vanilla

INGREDIENT NOTE

If walnuts are out of season, you can get them cheaply over the Internet; just type "buy nuts" or "buy walnuts" in your favorite search engine. Remember that you need the unshelled kind.

GARNISHES:

Apple slices

Peanut butter

INSTRUCTIONS:

Before you start, rinse off the walnuts. If you bought them in a mesh bag this is easy—just jiggle the bag under the shower for a minute or two. Sort out any split or badly cracked nuts and throw them away. Finally, prepare yourself a plate of apple slices smeared with peanut butter—or any snack you once loved but haven't eaten in years—to munch on while you're in the tub.

Now run a bath and add the almond oil, walnut extract, and vanilla. (A vanilla bean is not technically a nut, but it smells like one and is close enough to count.)

Add the walnuts last. Three pounds—that's about a hundred walnuts—is the minimum you'll want for an average-sized tub, but five pounds is better. The nuts will float in the water, and are a fun alternative to bubbles.

Make room for yourself and climb in, making sure there aren't too many behind you before you lean against the back of the tub. Now either sit back and relish the silliness of it all, or go ahead and enjoy your multitude of bobbing bath toys. Try fishing them out of the water using only your toes. Put a few under the sole of each foot and roll them along the bottom of the tub. Balance them on your head. If anyone knocks on the door and asks where all the clink clink noises are coming from, just yell "I am Count Oog Oog Oog!" and let them wonder.

Tiki Tub

— IF YOU LIKE PIÑA COLADAS —

The best time for a Tiki party is over the winter holidays. The days are short and cold, scratchy turtlenecks are everywhere, and the constant barrage of jingle bells and flashing lights have driven you insane. Try some tiki lights instead. Hold a ukulele-playing contest. Hollow out some coconuts and serve piña coladas, but drop in a paper umbrella and call them Tipi Tuki Tukis instead.

The problem is, not everyone understands the wintertime Tiki concept. Chances are, half your guests would show up wearing snowman earrings and some would decline to wear even a lei. Frustrated? Put on some sunglasses and a floppy straw hat and try this bath instead.

1 can coconut milk

3 tablespoons baking soda

Shot of rum, if desired

1½ cups pineapple juice,
  or 3 capfuls pineapple extract.

INGREDIENT NOTE

You'll find canned coconut milk in the Thai section of the market. Always shake the can before buying it. If it sloshes, it's good. If it doesn't slosh, that means the coconut milk has hardened inside and will be a poor choice for a bath.

GARNISHES:

Don Ho music

Jar of maraschino cherries

INSTRUCTIONS:

Play some Don Ho. It's really worth buying this music—there is just something delicious about listening to "Tiny Bubbles" during a Tiki bath. Shake the can of coconut milk thoroughly before opening, then pour it into a running bath. Add the baking soda, then the pineapple juice, or three capfuls of pineapple extract. If you don't want a virgin bath, throw in a shot of rum. Pop open a jar of maraschino cherries and eat them with your fingers, singing the Tiki Song:

The Tiki Song

(Begin with these words, then make up your own)
Kippi kippi tiki
A lua lua loma boa boa
Kippi kippi tiki
A boa boa lua . . . (etc.)

TUB TRIVIA

You don't need to know this, but you'll sound smart if you inform your friends that coconut milk is not actually the liquid from the middle from the coconut. It's made by steeping coconut flesh in water, a process almost like making coconut coffee.

The Bath Gourmet

Cream Soda Soak

— FOR LOVERS OF CREAM SODA —

There's just something about cream soda. When asked to be recipe testers for this book, several people immediately asked the same question: "Is there a cream soda bath? I want to test that one." Who knew there were so many passionate cream soda lovers out there? Or how persistent they could be? ("Sorry, no cream soda bath." "Pleeease?" "I don't think so." "PLEEEEASE?") Thus, after months of begging, a recipe just for those cream soda addicts who appreciate a bit of sweetness and fizz in their baths.

INGREDIENTS:

1 can cream soda, preferably sugarless
3 tablespoons vanilla
1 tablespoon cornstarch

GARNISHES:

Another can of cream soda to drink while bathing.

INSTRUCTIONS:

Add all three ingredients to a warm bath. You'll get the most out of the cream soda smell if you pour it and the vanilla directly under the faucet while the bath is running. Enter. Inhale. Soak. Sit. Enjoy your cream soda universe. And keep a spare can of cream soda on hand to drink in case the aroma of the bath tempts you too much.

Jello Bath for Two

— EVERYONE SHOULD TRY IT ONCE —

A Jello bath is one of those things that many have heard of but few are nervy enough to try. The thought of shoveling gallons of solidified gelatin out of the tub afterward, or needing an expensive plumber to come suck the jiggly stuff out of the pipes kills the idea for most people. Fortunately, all that trouble is unnecessary. You can get the feeling of a Jello bath without literally squishing through a tub of solidified gelatin. It's all about texture, and just a few packets of gelatin are enough for a unique bath experience— slick, slippery water, a terrific smell, and bragging rights forever.

INGREDIENTS:

6–7 packets Jello powder, preferably sugarless.

You're not going to be eating this Jello, so select your powder by scent, not flavor. Red powders in the tub can look like something out of a horror movie, so consider purples instead if you want a berry scent.

GARNISHES:

Ice cubes

INSTRUCTIONS:

Gelatin dissolves best in warm water, and sets best in cool. Therefore, choose your starting temperature according to personal comfort and by how long you'll be staying in the tub, though the starting temperature should not be very much warmer than body temperature. The idea is to add the powder, get in the tub, invite your partner, and then feel it slicken around you both as the water cools over the next fifteen minutes or so. Adding some ice cubes to the water speeds this process.

Ignore the temptation to lick the bath water off of any fingers or toes. However, if you have any extra powder left in the envelopes, you can mix it with small amounts of very hot water to make a tasty body paint.

PIONEER JELLO

Make your own flavored gelatin. It's just as easy and is much healthier than the prepackaged stuff. Add one package of unflavored gelatin to a cup of boiling water. Add between one and two cups of **clear** fruit juice (apple, grape, pineapple, or whatever) and, if you like, sugar to taste. Pour into small cups or bowls and refrigerate until firm.

Recipe Title: _____

Purpose: _____

Description: _____

Ingredients: _____

_____

Utensils: _____

Garnishes: _____

Instructions: _____

_____

_____

_____

_____

_____

Recipe Title: _____

Purpose: _____

Description: _____

Ingredients: _____

_____

Utensils: _____

Garnishes: _____

Instructions: _____

_____

_____

_____

_____

_____

Escape-It-All Baths

(AS IN: BATHS THAT WILL MAKE YOU LAUGH, SEND YOU ON A PRETEND VACATION, FOSTER YOUR INDEPENDENT SPIRIT, CURE A BAD MOOD, MAKE YOU FEEL LIKE A MOVIE STAR, GIVE YOU BRAGGING RIGHTS, ETC.)

Pirate Bath

Arrrrggh! Feel wicked? Nasty? Been stomping around and gnashing your teeth all day? Don't apologize—sometimes it's good to be a pirate. Enjoy your pirate self, feel as depraved as you please, and come out of the whole thing with sea-air skin, looking and feeling great. The rum scent is sure to indulge your mood, while the salt does its work smoothing your skin

It's possible that after this bath, you may look great but still feel like a pirate. That's okay, too. Go eat some ribs with your fingers, snarl at anyone who looks at you funny, then stomp back into the bathroom to fill another tub. Why not?

½ cup Epsom salt

1 tablespoon coconut oil

5 capfuls imitation rum extract, or ¾ cup rum

Raunchy novel (or cheap murder mystery, or anything that makes you feel depraved)

Pile of gold chocolate coins

Lock the bathroom door. Add the salt, coconut oil, and rum to a warm bath. Get in, lie back, and enjoy the naughtiness of it all. Read a trashy novel while eating gold chocolate coins. Roar if anyone tries to disturb you. Sing "Yo Ho Ho and a Bottle of Rum!" at the top of your voice. Sing even louder if anyone complains. Dare them to try pick the lock on the door. Douse them with water if they succeed.

Emerge when you're good and ready. Repeat as often as you please.

SHINY PIRATE HAIR

Mix up two or three egg yolks with another shot of the rum and rub into your hair. Leave it on while you bathe (wrapping your head in an old towel will help) and rinse thoroughly with cool water when you're done.

BOUNCY PIRATE HAIR

Sometime before your bath, open a bottle of beer (not a can) and allow it to go flat. Then, after you wash your hair, bend over and empty the beer slowly over your head, rubbing it into your hair as you go. It's much easier if a friend or shipmate helps you with this part. Rinse. Dry. Fluff.

Backrub Bath

— WHEN YOU CAN'T GET TO A SPA —

Everyone loves a backrub. A fancy one, in a sage-scented spa with exotic music plunking in the background, while a masseuse with enchanting fingers keeps all your unrubbed parts draped under a soothing warm sheet. But sometimes your credit card is already maxed, or your appointment isn't until three weeks from Monday, or you just are tired or sore and need some relief now.

This bath is particularly helpful if it is six in the morning, your body feels creaky, and no one is exactly volunteering to give you the full spa treatment at home. For this to work best, you need a tub with an attached shower. (If you don't have one, you could try faking it with one of those handheld showerhead attachments, but it won't work nearly as well.)

INGREDIENTS:
2 tablespoons vanilla

UTENSILS:
Tub with connected shower
Long-handled bath brush

GARNISHES:
Floating candles
Brand new (or at least very clean) robe

If you can't be in a spa, at least you can pretend. Unplug the phone and lock the bathroom door. Fill the sink and drop in some floating candles so you can bathe by candlelight. Cut the tags off a brand-new, never-worn robe and hang it invitingly on the back of the door.

Adjust the showerhead to a medium or narrow stream. Turn on a warm shower and close the drain. Kneel in the tub, so the stream hits your back as it gradually fills the bath. You can move forward or back to move the stream on and off your neck, and adjust the water pressure to whatever feels best. Rub with the bath brush also, up and down your spine and neck.

By the time the tub is full, your back should be feeling great. (If it isn't quite, then pop open the drain and run the shower for a few extra minutes.) When you're ready, pour two tablespoons of vanilla in the bath and soak. And remember, if anyone disturbs your tranquility, you are reasonably entitled to start the whole thing over from scratch—or get a free backrub!

SHOPPING NOTE

Invest in a high-quality bath brush. If you already have a cheap plastic (probably cracked) or wood (probably mildewed) one, throw it away now. The handle of a good brush will fit your hand just so, and the bristles will have exactly the right amount of give against your skin. It will make you feel pampered. The cheap kind will just make you feel yuck.

Act Your Shoe Size Bath

Have you seen those obnoxious birthday cards that ask: "Isn't it time to start acting your age, not your shoe size?" They have it all wrong. It's time to start acting your shoe size. Remember when taking a bath wasn't about "stress release" or "detoxification" or "aromatherapy"? It was about finally having the chance to play with the plastic submarine you got from a box of Loopy Crispies.

If you've caught yourself complaining about the latest tax changes during dinner, ruining a work shirt while you change a flat tire, or spending forty minutes on hold with your credit card company to debate a finance charge, then you need this bath!

1 packet Kool-Aid powder, or
½ packet Jello powder, in
your favorite color and scent

¼ cup baby oil
3 capfuls extra-mild bubble bath

GARNISHES:

Children's music

Bath toys (substitute three or
four half-inflated party balloons
if you don't have toys)

Bright towels and washcloth

Extra towel (to mop up the
bathwater you will slosh
onto the floor)

GARNISH NOTE

Don't skimp! The more the better.

INSTRUCTIONS:

Play some children's music. Set your player on "Repeat" so you will not
have to get out of the tub when the music runs out. Start running a warm
bath. Test frequently, like Goldilocks: not too hot, not too cold. Add the
Kool-Aid powder, baby oil, and bath toys. Climb in.

Add bubble bath. Check the recommended amount on the bottle, and
roughly double it. The idea is to have mounds of bubbles. You should be
able to construct a Mount Kilimanjaro of bubbles by the time you turn off
the water. When tub is full, sprinkle on more bath toys.

Play. Splash. Put bubbles in your hair. Don't wash behind your ears.
Wash twice between your toes. Watch your fingers prune up. Laugh too
loud. Sing too loud. Stay in too long.

UN-PIZZA MASK

One bad thing about youth is acne breakouts. To stop them in their tracks, smash a tomato into a bowl and squeeze in the juice from half of a lemon. (It is cheating and ineffective to substitute spaghetti sauce for the tomato.) Stir well. Goop onto your face, focusing on any acne-prone areas, and let the mixture do its work for ten minutes before rinsing.

Swamp Thing Bath

— BE A BOTANICAL GENIUS —

You would love to have a home filled with lush, green plants, but when you bring them home, things go wrong. Leaves develop black spots, or turn yellow, or drop off. Stems droop. Ants set up colonies in the soil. Before you know it, you're throwing away another pot of dirt with nothing but a withered stick poking out. Sound familiar? Believe it or not, this bath will ensure healthy green plants in your bathroom, at least.

In theory, air plants get all the moisture they need through the air—but that theory assumes they're living in a rain forest. The guy at the nursery will suggest spraying them every few days with a spray bottle, but that makes a mess, and you'll probably do it three or four times and then start forgetting. It's much easier to take the plants into the bath with you. They'll soak up some water, stay green and healthy, and occasionally sprout a long stem with a flower or two, to prove how well you're doing. Your friends will be dazzled, and you never, ever have to reveal the secret of your genius.

INGREDIENTS:

Air plants (epiphytes)

INGREDIENT NOTE

Air plants are those rootless, spiky little plants that you sometimes find glued inside the mouths of ceramic frogs, or wired to decorative bits of driftwood. Get the plants that look like little green hedgehogs, not the kind with flat leaves. You can usually find larger versions, not glued to anything, in nurseries. These are the ones you want, a whole bunch of them, but if your only option is prying the bitty ones out of the ceramic frogs, they'll work also.

GARNISHES:

Humongous gardening book (so everyone will think you slaved for your success).

INSTRUCTIONS:

Run a warm (not hot) bath. Including a few mild ingredients in the bath is all right, but never use salt or bubbles. Gather the air plants and drop them in the tub. They'll float like happy little bath toys while you bathe, and when you are done you can arrange them in baskets, or loose around the sink, or however your imagination dictates. A bowl of them makes a great centerpiece on a dinner table—just don't let anyone mistake them for a salad.

BRAND NEW PLANTS

Before using the plants for the first time, soak them in the sink for about twenty minutes and then gently rub the leaves to remove any residual dust or chemicals from the nursery.

INSTANT GREEN THUMB

If you are the kind of person who likes houseplants but never bothers with anything as fancy as fertilizer, try this: the next time you open a can of vegetables, don't pour the leftover green water down the drain—pour it in a houseplant instead to get instant fertilizer and an extra watering, all at once! (This also works with the leftover water after you've warmed or boiled vegetables on the stove.)

The Bath Gourmet

Ultimate Seduction Rose Bath

— DELIGHT —

You may have seen this one in the movies. Or in your fantasies. A rose petal bath isn't exactly practical for everyday, but you'll never feel more pampered, more spoiled, or more like an old-time movie star. Can you really live your whole life without trying this at least once?

INGREDIENTS:

One dozen (or more) large red roses

INGREDIENT NOTE

To get less-expensive roses, try buying them at the end of the day, when the florist might be throwing out the older bouquets. You can also ask if there are any older or damaged roses that you can have at a discount. Most florists will oblige, especially if business is slow.

UTENSILS:

Small pot with a lid
Strainer

GARNISHES:

Candles
Bath mask, or washcloth
Partner with camera

INSTRUCTIONS:

Before running the bath, boil the inner petals from one or two of the roses in a small, covered pot of water for five minutes. Cool and strain, retaining the petal-water. While the tub fills, add the petal-water, strip the petals from the remaining roses, turn off the lights, and light the candles. Enter the bath when it is full, and then sprinkle the petals into the tub around you. Lounge. Fantasize. Drape your arm over the edge of the tub like a movie star. A mask or folded washcloth over your eyes make you feel even more pampered; just be sure to lift the edge and peer at the rose petals any time your mood needs boosting.

If you are inclined, invite a partner to take a picture. You and your partner are both guaranteed to love a photo of yourself in this bath. And there's a bonus: after your photo session, your partner might be inspired to join you in the tub.

PETAL WATER NOTE

This smells a bit odd while boiling, but it's odorless and colorless in your tub . . . and it will keep a delicious, slightly tangy rose petal smell lingering on your skin after the bath. You'll be surprised!

Fingerpaint Tub

— CHEAPER THAN COUPLE'S THERAPY —

Couples need to play. If too many of your conversations involve where the phone book is and when the last time you had the oil changed was, you're not playing enough. There are lots of things you could try, but nothing in the world has the same tempting possibilities as a mountain of foamy body paints . . . and what happens afterward is up to you.

INGREDIENTS:

Shaving cream   Food coloring

UTENSILS:

Aluminum foil or plastic wrap   Old toothbrush (optional)

GARNISHES:

Lipstick   Water pistols

INSTRUCTIONS:

Spread a sheet of aluminum foil or plastic wrap on the side of the tub. Squirt on a few small piles of shaving cream, then add a drop or so of food coloring to each pile. Stir to blend each pile, either with your fingers or with the handle of an old toothbrush. Add more foam for lighter color, more coloring for darker. Mix for extra shades. Once your palette is ready, draw a few designs in the bathtub with lipstick to set the mood, then bring in your partner and get started.

Here's the Rule for Painting: you are only allowed to paint the other person, never yourself. Try a stripe down center of the nose. Knees are great locations for spirals or stars. Belly buttons are noses if you paint eyes on either side, or they're the centers of suns if you surround them with yellow rays. Or just go for head-to-toe tiger stripes, in bright orange, or maybe blue or red or green. Paint on arm bands. Squirt extra foam—without dye—on your heads and make hats, or ears, or dreadlocks. Now, run a bath.

Here's the Rule for Rinsing: you are only allowed to rinse the other person, never yourself. Splash one another, pour water over your heads, spray off the foam with water pistols, wipe off all those tiger stripes or lightning bolts or whatever has appeared. And that's it, no more rules . . . unless you're sad that the fun has ended. In that case, squirt more shaving cream and start again with the Rule for Painting.

MESS ALERT

To remove food coloring stains from your fingers, wash your hands with toothpaste or lemon juice.

Tropical Vacation Bath

— YOU NEED AN ESCAPE —

This last-resort bath is primarily used as an antidote for short, gray winter days, though it's equally effective against traffic jams, long hours, crowded parking lots, and sticky kitchen floors . . . as well as general boredom, lack of inspiration, malaise, or crabbiness. In other words, welcome to your one-hour tropical vacation.

The pineapple and salt will detoxify your skin as they transport your mind to an island paradise. Kool-Aid powder gives your bath water that amazing turquoise ocean color found only in the tropics.

1 packet blue Kool-Aid powder
   (Ice Blue Raspberry Lemonade
   flavor works well)
1 cup pineapple juice, or
   3 capfuls pineapple extract

1 tablespoon coconut oil
¼ cup Epsom salt
Banana slices for eyes

GARNISHES:

Calypso music
A few large Gerbera daisies, or
   a handful of large green leaves

Trashy "vacation" novel
Candles

INSTRUCTIONS:

Take the phone off the hook and lock the bathroom door. Make sure any-one at home knows not to disturb you. You are going to the tropics.

A body-temperature bath is ideal; think of warm tropical beaches. While the water is running, add the Kool-Aid, pineapple juice, coconut oil, and salt. If you want an even more tropical feel, double the salt. Play Calypso music, enter tub, and float Gerbera heads or greenery all around you. Read the kind of novel you save for vacations. Imagine you are bobbing in the turquoise waters of some far-away island.

Turn off lights and light candles. Pretend they are tiki torches. Banana slices on your eyelids are as good as cucumbers for reducing puffiness, and smell better. Eat the rest of the banana, or mash it into your hair for the duration of the bath; bananas are great for adding shine and moisture. After your bath, shower or rinse with fresh water, just as you would after a day at the beach.

JAMAICAN BANANA OMELET

Ever had a meal while you take a bath? This recipe from my Jamaican honeymoon is the one to try. Slice a banana into thin disks, put in a warm pan, and push to the side. They will cook while you prepare the rest of the omelet, especially if you remember to move them around occasionally; the key is to make sure the bananas are warm and soft before moving them into the omelet. Mix two eggs with a splash of milk and pour into pan. When eggs begin to harden, fold the banana into the omelet the usual way, add cheese and a pinch of cinnamon, and cook on both sides. Don't burn.

The Bath Gourmet

Bathaerobics

Exercise is not boring. Exercise done wrong is boring. Exercise as something serious, alone, solemn, in baggy clothes under fluorescent lights, is boring. You're most likely to stick with exercise if it's part of something you already enjoy, such as playing Frisbee with your dog, hiking with a friend, or soaking in a bath. You've heard of water aerobics. Here's the at-home version.

UTENSILS:

Lots of extra towels   Workout music

GARNISHES:

Sport drink

INSTRUCTIONS:

Start by spreading some extra towels around the base of the tub. A proper bath workout involves a few tidal waves, and you'll need the towels to soak up the mess. Play some workout music to get you in the mood. Run a warm bath, adding any extra ingredients you like. Soak for a while, letting the heat loosen your muscles, and then start the workout. Do the exercises in order, repeating each one until you're tired.

Stretches

Foot to Face: Brace your shoulders against the back of the tub and one of your feet against the front, so you won't slide around. Grab the heel of your free foot and bring it as close to your face as possible. Hold a few seconds, release, repeat, then do the same with the other leg.

Foot to Ceiling: Still holding your heel from the Foot to Face exercise, straighten your leg toward the ceiling. Let your hands slide down to your calves if you have to, just get your leg as straight as possible. Hold a few seconds, release, repeat, then do the same with the other leg.

Cardio

Water Bike: Rest your head on the back of the tub and prop yourself up on your elbows. Bicycle your legs in the air over the water. If you slide down, move back up and continue. Done correctly, this will produce your first tidal wave; don't worry about it, that's what the towels are for. When you're done, add more water to the tub.

Strength

Hover Legs: Lean your head on the back of the tub and start with both legs straight up in the air. Lower them to about the height of the faucet (or as low as you can without bumping into the wall) and hold there. Breathe. Hold for the slow count of ten before releasing, and then repeat.

Bath Crunch: Rest in a loose "V" position, with your head and feet propped on the ends of the tub. Crunch, bringing your chest and thighs together in the middle, so you are upright and balanced on your bottom. It's cheating to use your hands. Repeat. Repeat. Repeat. This also creates a tidal wave, but it is your grand finale, so go for it!

Polar Bear Bath

— FOR THRILL SEEKERS WITH TWO TUBS —

Wherever it gets really cold, a certain type of daredevil will emerge. These are the people who strip off their clothes in the snow, then leap as a group into icy water, bobbing like grinning penguins for a minute before sprinting into a nearby sauna. Sound exciting? Many claim that this is one of the best things you can do for your circulatory system. Others swear that it tightens your skin and helps erase wrinkles. Warm climate types do the same thing with "cold plunges"—a small tub of icy water to dunk yourself in before lunging into a hot tub. The sensation is exceptional, like a tingling envelope of warmth once you enter the heated water. Ready to try?

Ice cubes

Two bathtubs
Slippers or sandals with plenty of traction
Extra towels

Candles

Fill the cold tub first. Run water from the cold tap only. Empty a tray of ice cubes into the water—if you're going to do this, you might as well do it all the way! Don't forget to spread some extra towels on the floor around the tub, and leave a pair of slippers at the edge. Run a hot bath in the second tub. Light a few candles around the rim, for ambiance, and you're ready to go.

Jump in the cold tub. Dunk yourself completely under water, hold there for four seconds, then leap out. Pull on slippers! Run! Sprint like mad down the hall into the warm tub. Scramble into the water, then sink down to your chin and enjoy your victory. When you're ready, don't forget to re-light the candles you splashed out on your way into the tub.

SAFETY NOTE

Don't forget the slippers. Frantic, wet, and naked can lead to some spectacular falls otherwise.

Outdoor Bath

— FOR A CHANGE —

It's hot. You don't have access to a pool. You're also sweaty, and you probably need a bath. Not in the mood? An outdoor bath can be a lot more fun than an indoor one on a hot summer afternoon, and there is absolutely no reason not to try it. (This one's so obvious, it's surprising more people don't think of it for themselves.)

INGREDIENTS:
Mild soap & washcloth

UTENSILS:
Swimsuit
Plastic kiddie pool, or outdoor laundry tub
Hose

Sprinkler

Put on a swimsuit and drag your kiddie pool or plastic tub into your backyard or driveway. The driveway is better because it allows you to dump the water directly into the sewer afterward, but you might want a little more privacy. Or not.

If you're feeling brave, turn on the hose, step in the kiddie pool, and fill by holding the hose over your head. If you're not quite that hardy, fill the tub with the hose and add two pots of hot water from an inside tap before you jump in. Bathe. Use a small amount of mild soap that will be bio-friendly when you dump out the bath at the end. Wash your hair also, and rinse with the hose. Ignore the stares of the neighbors. Who cares what they think?

Let your dog in the tub if he wants to join you. He probably needs to get clean, also. When you're done, you can both rinse off under your sprinkler, if you have one, or the hose if you don't.

WARNING

Don't use salt, oil, or any other ingredient that will be toxic to plants when you splash the water around. (If you can't splash, what's the point?)

ANOTHER WARNING

Don't bathe in a hot tub. The soap will probably destroy the jets. At best, it will linger in the pipes and you will get foam every time you run the hot tub forevermore.

Bare Cupboard Bath

You're out of milk. And tea bags. And oranges. And who really keeps mustard powder in the house, anyway? And you don't feel like driving all the way to the store, but you're in the mood for a bath and mere water is just too boring. You are too marvelous for that. You deserve better! You have a few options: you can send the butler to the market, you can light a candle and fake it, or you can try this bath.

INGREDIENTS:

2 capfuls mint-scented mouthwash

3 squirts liquid soap

Salt from old takeout packages,
   if desired

A splash of any cooking oil,
   if desired

GARNISHES:

Dishwashing liquid

Small bowl

INSTRUCTIONS:

It's not glamorous but it works. Two capfuls of mint-scented mouthwash and three squirts of mild liquid soap into a running bath will pass for a foamy, minty bathstravaganza, at least until you can get to the store. Adding a splash of oil or a handful of salt make it even better, and are even good for your skin.

Squirt some dishwashing liquid into a small bowl on the side of the tub. Go ahead and soak your fingers during your bath; most dishwashing liquids include extra ingredients to condition your skin. You can enjoy the benefit without doing the work. Don't tell.

EMERGENCY SHAMPOO

Your hair looks scary but you're out of time or shampoo?
This sounds odd but it works: stand in the tub (this is
messy) and sprinkle a fat pinch of cornstarch into a
hairbrush. Brush the cornstarch through your hair,
remembering the undersides. If you have long hair, repeat
once or twice. Give the cornstarch a few minutes to absorb
the greasies while you rinse out your brush and wash
the cornstarch off your nose. Now brush just enough to
remove all visible powder from your hair. Viola!

Cinderella Warning: Your hair will be super for about eight
hours, and then, **poof,** will go back to being scary all at
once. If you're going to be out longer, bring along a brush
and a little baggie of cornstarch.

Recipe Title:

Purpose:

Description:

Ingredients:

Utensils:

Garnishes:

Instructions:

Recipe Title:

Purpose:

Description:

Ingredients:

Utensils:

Garnishes:

Instructions:

Recipe Title: _____
Purpose: _____
Description: _____
Ingredients: _____

_____
Utensils: _____
Garnishes: _____
Instructions: _____

_____
_____
_____
_____

Recipe Title: _____
Purpose: _____
Description: _____
Ingredients: _____

_____
Utensils: _____
Garnishes: _____
Instructions: _____

_____
_____
_____
_____

Bath à la Carte

(DESIGN-IT-YOURSELF BATH SUGGESTIONS

FOR INDEPENDENT TYPES)

Bath à la Carte

When a sign points in one direction, there are certain people who always feel compelled to explore the other. These are the same people who blaze new trails, who eat the most outrageous thing on the menu, who discover dinosaur bones in their own backyards while digging their own holes to China. If you're one of those people, you probably want the chance to design your own super-bath as well. Just follow the five steps below to design your own, personalized bath.

Naturally, as an independent type, you are liable to decide to add steps, skip steps, or come up with your own ingredients. You may decide to bathe in potato chips instead of water. Who knows? Just be sure to choose ingredients that won't stain your skin or tub (like ink or pomegranate juice), won't clog your drain (like mud or catsup) and are mild enough not to irritate your skin or corrode your plumbing. Enjoy!

Step One: Pick a base

Milky Base	Oily Base	Salty Base
2 cups whole or powdered milk	1 tablespoon baby, almond, coconut, or apricot oil	½ cup salt

Step Two: Add a counterpart

Smooth Counterpart	Sweet Counterpart	Soft Counterpart
⅓ cup cornstarch	2–3 tablespoons vanilla	1 tablespoon honey

The Bath Gourmet

Step Three: Get crazy

This is where things get interesting. Choose one or more items from any of the lists below:

Ingredients That Must Be Squeezed Into the Tub:

Grapefruit	Lime
Lemon	Orange

Ingredients That Must Be Steeped Into the Tub:

Ground ginger	Oatmeal
Lavender	Rice
Mint leaves	Rosemary

Ingredients That Can Be Added Directly To the Tub:

Cinnamon sticks	Ginger powder
Cucumber slices	Jello powder
Essential oil (any scent)	Mustard powder
Extract (pineapple/walnut/	Seltzer water
coconut/banana/etc.)	Tea bags

Step Four: Top it off

Add a few drops of food coloring, a capful of bubble bath, or both.

Step Five: Name and record your creation

Is it Irene's Rice Milk Surprise? Or maybe it's the Adele Loves Apricots Bath, or even Tony's Tempting Tea Tub. Half the fun is the name, so choose well. Then, record your creation on the special recipe card pages so you can recreate it next time!

Bath
Crafts

(AS IN: BATH SALT, BATH OIL, FIZZY BOMBS,

FOAMY MELTS, DINOSAUR EGGS AND

OTHER ENTERTAINING STUFF THAT

YOU MAKE YOURSELF)

Homemade Bath Salts

The first trick while making bath salts is in managing the proportions of the ingredients. The measurements listed here are meant as starting points only—experiment with various amounts of essential oil and food coloring for results to your taste. The second trick is to store the salts in a closed jar. Stray splashes from the shower or tub, or even the humidity from a hot shower, can transform the salt into a solid clump if left exposed.

Simple Salt

3 cups Epsom salt, rock salt,
   or sea salt
9–10 drops essential oil in your
   choice of fragrance

Food coloring (optional)
Glass jar with lid

Put the salt in a mixing bowl. Stir in the essential oil, just one or two drops at a time. It's okay if a small amount of the salt dissolves during this process, but if all of your salt melts away, you've used too much oil. Now stir in a small amount of food coloring—again, start with just a drop or two and go from there. Spread the mixture on clean paper towels (or a sheet of aluminum foil) to dry overnight, then store in a closed jar.

Use two heaping tablespoons per bath.

Super Salt

3 cups Epsom salt, rock salt, or sea salt

1 tablespoon powdered milk

1 teaspoon any light oil

4–5 drops essential oil of your choice

2–3 drops food coloring

Glass jar with lid

1 teaspoon Vitamin E oil (optional)

Put the salt and powdered milk in a large, shallow mixing bowl. Stir in the light oil a drop or so at a time. The essential oil, food coloring and Vitamin E oil should be added last. This mixture will take a day or so to dry—hurry the process by spreading it on clean paper towels or a sheet or aluminum foil. Store in a closed glass jar.

Homemade Bath Oils

True, you could just dump baby oil into the tub and call it finished, but these recipes feel better. Much better. Extra ingredients like honey, salt, and milk work with the oil to make you as sleek as an otter—people will line up just to touch your skin after taking one of these baths. (And if this doesn't literally happen, know that people secretly want to but are too shy or jealous.)

Easy Peasy Oil

¼ cup baby oil

1 cup milk

⅓ cup baking soda

2–3 drops essential oil of your choice (optional)

1 capful baby bubble bath (optional)

Mix all ingredients in a mixing bowl or blender. That's it.

Makes one bath. Double or triple the amounts if you want extra to store for later, or better yet, make the Fancy Schmancy oil and store that instead.

MESS ALERT

If adding bubble bath, stir it in separately after the other ingredients are mixed—do **not** put it in the blender.

Fancy Schmancy Oil

½ cup baby oil

3 tablespoons rum

1 cup salt

1 egg

½ cup milk

¼ cup baking soda

Mix or blend all ingredients thoroughly. This oil can be stored in a snazzy glass jar and kept by the tub—stick a few sprigs of something green and leafy in the jar to make it even fancier. A few splashes are enough for one bath. Shake before using.

Homemade Bath Bombs

— FIZZIES —

Bomb? What kind of book is this, anyway? Some people give you a blank—or alarmed—look when you start talking about bath bombs. To allay any fears: bath bombs are those expensive colored balls, usually about the size of a fist, often seen in bath shops. The ball is dropped in the tub and immediately begins to fizz, bubble and eventually dissolve, thereby filling the tub with color or scent or oil. Fancy stores sometimes call them "bath tablets" and promise that they will "effervesce," which is basically the same thing.

½ cup citric acid

1 cup baking soda

¼ cup cornstarch, or powdered
milk

1 tablespoon vanilla

Food coloring (optional)

Dry herbs (optional)

Light oil (optional)

Essential oil, any scent (optional)

Round or shaped 2-sided (closed)
molds, if desired (obtained in
craft stores or through online
soapmaking suppliers. Inexpensive
and recommended, especially
if you're making bath bombs
as gifts.)

INGREDIENT NOTE

Citric acid is inexpensive, but can be tricky to find. It is used in canning and preserves—it prevents cut fruit from turning brown—and also for soap-making. The easiest way to get some is to type "purchase citric acid" or "soap-making supplies" into an Internet search engine and order it by the pound from an online store. You can also look for citric acid in the canning/preserving section of a market or drugstore. You shouldn't have to pay more than $3 or $4 a pound, which will last you a while.

INSTRUCTIONS:

Mix the citric acid, baking soda, and cornstarch in a dry mixing bowl. Make as much or little as you like, as long as the proportions are twice as much baking soda as citric acid, and twice as much citric acid as cornstarch. Very slowly, stir in no more than one tablespoon of vanilla, just a few drops at a time, and finish by adding one or two drops of food coloring. Your goal is to have a mixture that is as dry as possible, yet able to hold its form (barely) when pressed into a ball.

Add crushed dried herbs, light oil, or essential oil as you like. Remember, a little goes a long way!

Press the mixture into molds, or form into balls roughly the size of plums (or meatballs) and leave on waxed paper or aluminum foil to dry. They expand as they dry, so leave room between them; the more liquid you added to the mix, the more the bombs will expand and flatten. If they expand and flatten a lot, don't throw them away—try forming round tinfoil "cups" to contain them in the right shape. When they are fully dry, you can peel off the tinfoil and they'll still be effective, just not quite as fizzy as bombs made from a drier mixture.

The bombs will take between one and two days to dry thoroughly, longer if they're in a closed mold. Any contact with moisture can make them start fizzing, so if you want to keep them in the bathroom consider storing them in a closed container or wrapped individually in plastic wrap. (Try colored plastic wrap if you want to get fancy.)

FIELD NOTE

Try making a half-sized batch the first time, while you get the hang of the process. Try using 1 cup baking soda, ¼ cup citric acid, and ⅛ cup of cornstarch.

The Bath Gourmet

BATH BOMB GIFT IDEAS

LOVE NOTES
Type a brief love note (or write with waterproof ink) on a slip of colored paper and insert in the center of a bath bomb. When the bomb dissolves, the note will be exposed.

FORTUNES
As above, with fortunes.

CHARACTER BOMBS
Use a large felt-tip pen or highlighter to gently draw google eyes and bulby noses on the surfaces of dry bombs.

MONSTER BOMBS
As above, with green bombs.

JACK O'BOMBS
As above, with orange bombs.

DINOSAUR EGGS
Put a small plastic dinosaur in the center of each bomb. As the bomb dissolves, the dinosaur "hatches."

SNAKE EGGS
As above, with plastic or tiny rubber snakes.

NAVY SEAL STEALTH TIMED INFILTRATOR UNITS
Green bombs with plastic soldiers inside.

Homemade Bath Muffins

These are novelty bath bombs, not any trickier to make than the normal kind, but fun to give as gifts or to stack in a guest bathroom.

INGREDIENTS:

All ingredients required for a basic bath bomb (see Bath Bomb recipe)
Small dried cranberries or other dried berry (optional)
Essential oil in any "muffin-y" scent (berry varieties work best)
Muffin tin
Muffin papers
Food coloring

INSTRUCTIONS:

Follow the directions for creating bath bombs, but do not add food coloring to the initial mix. If you like, you can stir in a small amount of dried berries, to add to the muffin-like final effect. You may also substitute a few drops of essential oil for some of the vanilla while creating the mix.

Press your mixture firmly into each paper cup in the muffin tin. After an hour, the mix should have puffed slightly over the top of each cup. If the muffins have puffed too much, you probably added too much liquid to the mixture. The muffins will still be good, but may not fizz quite as much as they otherwise might have. Now is the time to add the food coloring if you want to create a frosted, cupcake-like appearance. Use just two or three drops of food coloring, carefully applied on the top of each muffin.

Allow one or two days to dry, then remove from cups with the muffin papers still on.

Homemade Bath Melts

— FOAMIES —

A bath melt, or foamie, is a bath bomb without the boom. Instead of violently fizzing away in a minute or two, a melt will putter around the surface of the water leaving an expanding foam trail behind as it slowly dissolves. The ingredients of bombs and melts are the same, only the proportions and preparation are different.

INGREDIENTS:

¾ cup citric acid

2 cups baking soda

¾ cup powdered milk

2 tablespoons vanilla

Food coloring

Dry herbs (optional)

Light oil (optional)

Essential oil, any scent (optional)

Round or shaped 2-sided (closed) molds (obtained in craft stores or through online soapmaking suppliers

INSTRUCTIONS:

Follow the directions for mixing the bath bombs, using the new proportions for the ingredients. Notice that you're using less of the citric acid (fizzy part) and more of the powdered milk (foamy part) than in the bath bomb recipe. When the mixture is just moist enough to hold together in balls, arrange on a cookie sheet. They will flatten and spread as they dry, ideally not to the degree that they will run together. Don't panic if that happens—you can snap them apart when they are fully dry. Next time, either use less liquid or make smaller balls. (You can also refer to the Bath Bomb and Bath Muffin recipes for other ideas of how to shape the balls.)

After a day or so, when they are fully dry, you can slide the "cookies" off the sheet. Try one out in the bath. Remember: this isn't an exact science, so if you want them foamier next time, use more powdered milk; if you want them fizzier, use more citric acid.

Appendices

Banana
Moisturizing, and rumored to have strong anti-aging and anti-wrinkle properties. Also a mild exfoliant.

Baking soda
The ultimate deodorizer. Also very refreshing, and excellent for balancing out acidic ingredients such as grapefruit or lemon.

Banana extract (imitation)
Adds the smell of bananas. Sold in little bottles, like vanilla, near the baking/spice section in the market.

Black tea
Anti-inflammatory, soothing.

Beer
Adds body to hair. Use bottled, not canned.

Bubble bath
Adds bubbles. Use mild types with few ingredients on the label, such as bubble bath intended for babies.

Chamomile tea
Reduces puffiness, soothes skin.

Cinnamon tea

Mild astringent and antiseptic, also considered an aphrodisiac.
Not recommended for pregnant women.

Citric acid

Puts the fizz in fizzy project recipes, like bath bombs. Sorry, can't be
substituted with any other ingredient.

Chocolate

No chocoholic can resist. Also an aphrodisiac. Use in powdered or syrup
form and mix with milk before adding to tub; makes a huge mess if added
to water directly. Instant hot chocolate powder generally won't work.

Coconut milk

Softens and moisturizes skin, also smells great. Can be used as a substitute
for cow's milk if necessary. Sold in cans. Note: this is not the watery liquid
found in the center of the coconut, so don't use that stuff.

Cornstarch

Softens skin. Cornstarch might leave a slight powder residue on the
bottom of your tub, but this can be easily brushed or blown away.

Cream soda

Great smell, also fun because it is fizzy. Use sugarless varieties if possible.

Cucumber

Reduces puffiness, cools skin, adds moisture. Also has a very slight
bleaching effect when applied directly to skin.

Egg

Moisturizing, also adds shine and body to hair.

Flowers
A nice extra touch if you like that sort of thing. Also use dried.

Ginger/ginger powder
Strong detoxifier and stimulant, widely considered to have healing properties. Also possibly good for cellulite.

Grapefruit
Detoxifies, energizes, smoothes skin. Acidic, so feel free to add a few tablespoons of baking soda to balance it out.

Honey
Gentle antiseptic and astringent, moisturizes, draws impurities out of the skin. Plain honey is best, but any variety is fine. Remember, solid additives in fancy honey won't dissolve in water.

Kool-Aid powder/Jello powder
Use sugarless varieties if possible. Both are ideal for adding color and a wide assortment of aromas. However, it's a bad idea to choose any deep red-tinted powder to a bath. The result looks alarmingly gory.
Note: It's rumored that the color in these powders can be absorbed by hair, especially if it is color-processed, so keep your hair out of the water.

Lavender
Soothes muscles, widely said to induce sleep.

Lemon
Detoxifies, mild stimulant. Fantastic for clearing sinuses. Mild bleaching effect, so keep your hair out of the water. Acidic, so toss in a few tablespoons of baking soda if you want to balance it out.

Maple flavoring (imitation)

Smells just like maple syrup, without clogging your drain. Found in the baking/spices section of the market.

Milk (liquid)

Use whole milk. Softens skin. For full effect, you should soak for twenty minutes or more in milk-based baths.

Milk (powdered)

Can be substituted for liquid milk. Use the instructions on the box to equate the amount of powder you use with the amount of liquid milk called for. Note: If powdered milk has changed color with age, or has a bad smell, don't use it. The odor will be magnified in the tub and your bath will smell like a diaper.

Mint

The fresher the better. Smells good, energizes.

Mustard powder

Detoxifies, sometimes thought to help with sleeplessness.

Oatmeal

Extremely soothing for itchy skin, rashes, and other skin problems. Also an exfoliant.

Oil

Baby, almond, coconut, sesame seed, apricot, etc. As a rule, the heavier the oil, the less of it you should use.

Orange/orange peel
Detoxifies. Some people are energized by the smell of oranges; this may be a chemical reaction, or simply a subconscious association with drinking orange juice in the morning. See if it works for you.

Pineapple/pineapple extract (imitation)
Detoxifies, also possibly an anti-inflammatory. Also refreshes skin. Pineapple is acidic, however, so if you have very sensitive skin you can substitute a few capfuls of pineapple extract—found in the baking/spice section of the market—and get the pineapple smell without the acid.

Rice
Extremely soothing, and softens skin. Instant white rice works best, though any variety is okay. Tip: If you don't usually buy rice, you can just grab a box of those boil-in-bag rice packets—each packet contains the precise amount you need for a bath.

Root beer concentrate
Irresistible to fans of root beer. Found in the baking/spice section of the market. Note: This is extremely concentrated, so use only a drop at a time.

Rosemary
Energizes.

Rum
Adds shine to hair, smells good. Note: You should never drink alcohol before or during a bath.

Rum extract (imitation)
Adds the smell of rum without using the real thing.

Salt

Relieves aches and pains, exfoliates, detoxifies, possibly reduces stress. Many people believe that salt baths have medicinal properties. There is no substitute for salt, but people with sensitive skin should read the salt warning in the beginning of this book. The recipes call for Epsom salt, although rock salt, sea salt, and especially Dead Sea salt are also excellent.

Seaweed

Detoxifies, energizes, moisturizes. Look for the dried sheets in the market.

Tomato

Mild astringent, acne fighter.

Vanilla

Excellent smell, also a good non-oily liquid base for homemade bath products.

Walnuts (unshelled)

Extremely buoyant bath toys.

Walnut extract (imitation)

Adds the smell of walnuts. Found in the baking/spice section of the market.

Yogurt

Use unflavored types. The acids in yogurt help restore natural acid levels in skin. Also acts as a moisturizer, and is a good base for mixing other ingredients.

APPENDIX B: INGREDIENTS BY CATEGORY

Use this chart when you want to substitute an ingredient or you're look-ing for Bath à la Carte ideas. For example, if a recipe includes grapefruit and you loathe grapefruit, you'd check this list and see that grapefruit is a detoxifier. You could then substitute a different detoxifier, such as an orange.

DETOXIFY	MOISTURIZE/SOFTEN SKIN	SOOTHE SKIN
Ginger/ginger powder	Banana	Black tea
Grapefruit	Coconut milk	Chamomile tea
Lemon	Cornstarch	Cucumber
Mustard powder	Egg	Oatmeal
Orange/orange peel	Milk/powdered milk	Rice
Pineapple/pineapple	Rice	
extract	Yogurt	
Salt		
Seaweed		

INDEX

Photo by Tony Van, taken at the Monde Spa
in Redwood Shores, California.

Rhonda Van is a freelance writer and artist who lives with her husband, Tony, in Redwood Shores, California. She knows three secrets: that people take themselves too seriously, how to make anything fun (including baths!), and one that she isn't telling.